DIGESTION
NUTRITION &
REPRODUCTION

by

STEVE PARKER

Consultant

DR KRISTINA ROUTH

HOW TO USE THIS BOOK

This book is your guide to yourself – an atlas of the human body. Follow the main text to get an informative overview of a particular area of the body, or use the boxes to jump to a specific area of interest. Finally, there are even experiments for you to try yourself!

Body Locator

The highlighted areas on the body locator tell you immediately which areas of the body you are learning about. This will help you to understand your body's geography.

Instant Facts

This box gives you snappy facts that summarise the topic in just a few sentences. Find out where your stomach actually is, how we are made and much more.

Healthwatch

Go here to read about illness and disease related to the relevant area of the body. For example, on the section about digestion, learn about why eating sometimes causes heartburn.

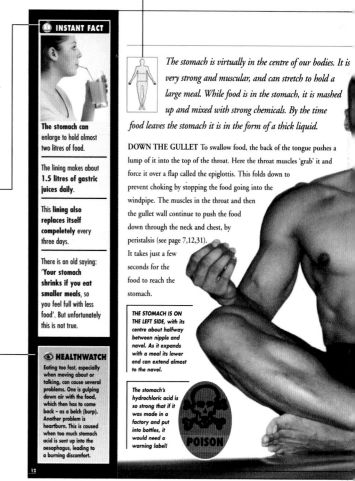

🌀 INSTANT FACT

The stomach can enlarge to hold almost two litres of food.

The lining makes about **1.5 litres of gastric juices daily.**

This lining also **replaces itself compeletely** every three days.

There is an old saying: 'Your stomach **shrinks if you eat smaller meals,** so you feel full with less food'. But unfortunately this is not true.

◉ HEALTHWATCH

Eating too fast, especially when moving about or talking, can cause several problems. One is gulping down air with the food, which then has to come back – as a belch (burp). Another problem is heartburn. This is caused when too much stomach acid is sent up into the oesophagus, leading to a burning discomfort.

The stomach is virtually in the centre of our bodies. It is very strong and muscular, and can stretch to hold a large meal. While food is in the stomach, it is mashed up and mixed with strong chemicals. By the time food leaves the stomach it is in the form of a thick liquid.

DOWN THE GULLET To swallow food, the back of the tongue pushes a lump of it into the top of the throat. Here the throat muscles 'grab' it and force it over a flap called the epiglottis. This folds down to prevent choking by stopping the food going into the windpipe. The muscles in the throat and then the gullet wall continue to push the food down through the neck and chest, by peristalsis (see page 7,12,31). It takes just a few seconds for the food to reach the stomach.

THE STOMACH IS ON THE LEFT SIDE, with its centre about halfway between nipple and navel. As it expands with a meal its lower end can extend almost to the navel.

The stomach's hydrochloric acid is so strong that if it was made in a factory and put into bottles, it would need a warning label!

POISON

12

🪶 Diagrams

Go to this box for scientific diagrams complete with annotations that tell you exactly what you are looking at.

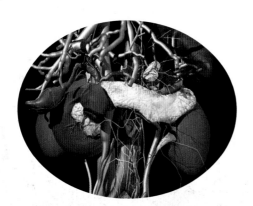

In Focus

This panel takes a really close look at one aspect of the human body, using stunningly detailed macro-imagery and stills taken from an anatomically correct digital model of human anatomy.

SQUEEZE AND SQUIRM The stomach is not just a stretchy bag that holds food before it passes to the next part of the digestive system. As it fills with a meal, the powerful layers of muscles in the stomach walls make it churn and squirm to squash the chewed food into a pulp. Also the stomach's lining releases a watery liquid called gastric juice. This attacks the food with powerful chemicals called acids and enzymes. The 'acid bath' of hydrochloric acid in the stomach also helps to kill germs that came in with the food.

Barium is a substance that shows up as pale or white on X-rays. A barium meal fills the inside of the stomach and shows its shape and position, to reveal problems like tightness or constriction.

DIGESTION, NUTRITION & REPRODUCTION

IN FOCUS
SWALLOWING

tongue

muscles

windpipe

The base of the tongue extends down into the neck and helps to push food into the gullet, which is behind the windpipe. The strap-like muscles around the upper windpipe and voicebox also help in swallowing.

TRY IT YOURSELF
Ask friends to point to where they think a stomach-ache would be. They may indicate around the navel (belly button). But you know better! The stomach is much higher, just behind the lower left ribs.

STOMACH WALL
The stomach lining has named regions and is wrinkled and folded (right). Around it are three layers of muscles, each with fibres arranged in a different directions.

Duodenum Cardiac Region

Gastric Body

Pyloric Region

Gastric Fundus

13

Try it Yourself

Activity boxes with exercises that you can try yourself. No special equipment required – just your own body!

INTRODUCTION

If your body was a spacecraft, then the modules for delivery of fresh supplies and waste removal would be your abdomen. This is the part of the body below the chest and above the legs. It contains the gurgling guts, bulging bladder and, in females more than males, the reproductive system too.

FOOD AND DRINK The digestive system breaks down foods and absorbs liquids for the body's nutritional and water-balance needs. The system begins well above the abdomen, at the mouth. When chewed food is swallowed into the abdomen, it passes through the long digestive passageway of the stomach, small intestine and large intestine. What comes out of the other end, at the base of the abdomen, is leftovers and unwanted material – one of several wastes that the body gets rid of every day.

WASTE DISPOSAL Another type of waste is removed by the urinary system. This has no direct connection with the digestive system. Its wastes are body byproducts and excess water filtered from the blood stream, as the liquid known as urine. This is stored in a stretchy bag, the bladder, until it is convenient for it to be expelled.

LONG-TERM SURVIVAL Unlike the digestive and urinary systems, the reproductive system is not essential for the survival of an individual. But it is vital for the long-term survival of our kind – the human species. In a woman, the reproductive system is contained in the abdomen, but in the man, the parts are positioned below it. The 'product' of the reproductive process is a helpless bundle which alternately feeds and gets rid of waste, as well as crying and sleeping – a baby.

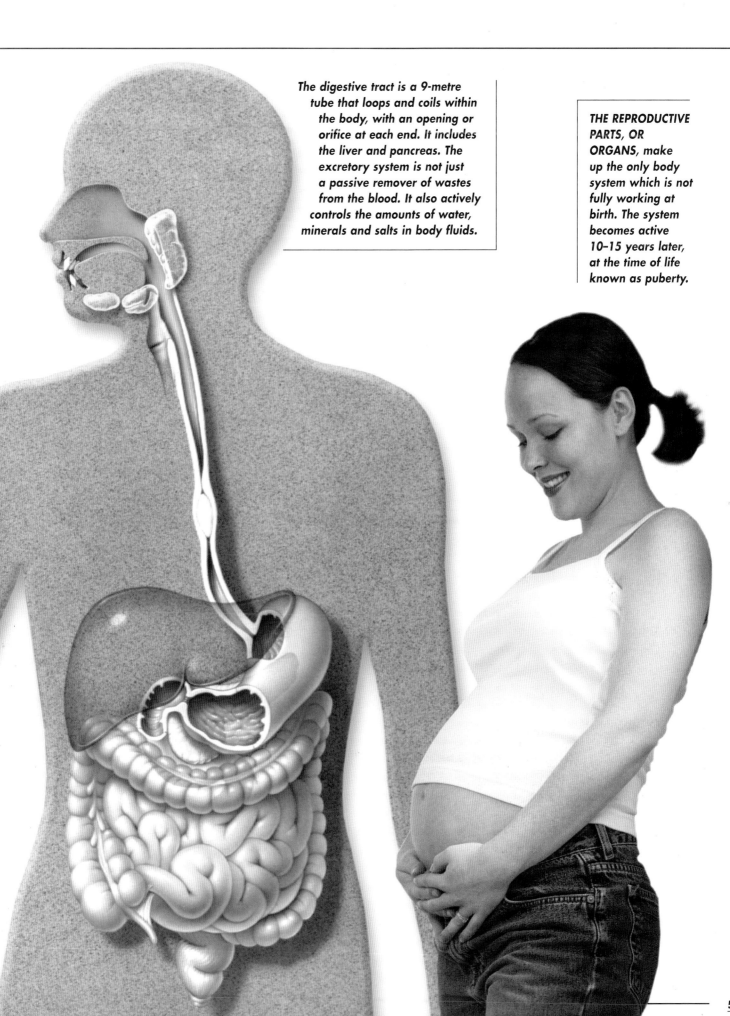

The digestive tract is a 9-metre tube that loops and coils within the body, with an opening or orifice at each end. It includes the liver and pancreas. The excretory system is not just a passive remover of wastes from the blood. It also actively controls the amounts of water, minerals and salts in body fluids.

THE REPRODUCTIVE PARTS, OR ORGANS, make up the only body system which is not fully working at birth. The system becomes active 10–15 years later, at the time of life known as puberty.

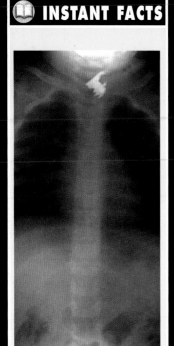

The **average length of the adult digestive tract** is about nine metres.

The stomach is about 30 cm around its curve. Food takes between **15 and 48 hours to digest.**

Our bodies need energy to stay active, and even to keep breathing.

DIGESTION *Digestive System*

When you swallow a well-chewed mouthful of food, after savouring its delicious flavours, that seems to be an end to the matter. But for the food, it is only the beginning. The digestive process is lengthy and complicated, as the food moves at an average speed of 30 centimetres per hour through the body.

GULP! The digestive system has about a dozen major parts which come into action one after the other. Food's first encounter with the body is the mouth. Here the teeth slice and crush it, the tongue tastes it and moves it around for thorough chewing, and the food is moistened with watery saliva from the salivary glands around the jaw. Next the food makes its way down the gullet (or oesophagus) which is a link pipe down through the chest, between the mouth above and the stomach below.

STOMACH & INTESTINES After a few hours being physically and chemically attacked in the stomach, the mashed food passes to the small intestine, which is very long, and folded and coiled to fit in the abdomen. The small intestine further breaks down or digests the food, and takes the nutrients your body needs into the blood stream.

IN FOCUS
SYSTEM OVERVIEW

Any food left over passes into the large intestine, where water is taken from it according to the body's needs. Finally, the wastes are compacted and stored in the rectum, before being expelled through the anus.

TRACT & SYSTEM The parts above form the digestive tract. But two more organs are vital for the whole digestive system. The pancreas makes powerful juices to aid chemical digestion and the liver receives most of the digestive nutrients from the small intestine. It stores, processes or releases these nutrients.

VAST AREAS OF LAND ARE USED TO GROW OUR FOOD. Farming, harvesting, processing, packing, transporting and selling the stuff that goes into our digestive systems, make up one of the world's largest industries.

IN A BIOGESTER (ABOVE RIGHT) LEFTOVER FOODS, garden wastes and similar material rot down and release a burnable gas called methane. The body's digestive system also releases burnable gases when it digests food.

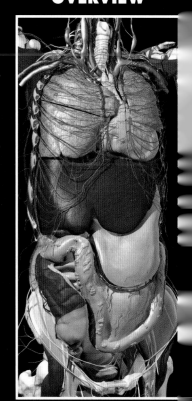

Most of the digestive tract is folded and packaged into the abdomen. It almost fills this largest of body cavities, dominated by the dark red liver and paler stomach.

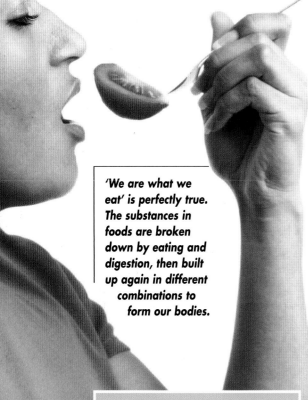

'We are what we eat' is perfectly true. The substances in foods are broken down by eating and digestion, then built up again in different combinations to form our bodies.

TRY IT YOURSELF

At your next meal, slow down slightly. Sit for a time before and after. Chew each mouthful 10 to 20 times. Savour the flavours and enjoy the textures, separately and combined.

PERISTALSIS AND DIGESTION

Due to pressure inside the body, food must be forced along the digestive tract. It is massaged along or pushed by peristalsis, which is wave-like contractions of the muscles in the tract wall. The process of digestion is carefully timed so that the parts of the tract become active one after the other, as food moves on its journey. This timing is controlled by nerve signals from the brain and 'messenger' chemicals, hormones, in the blood.

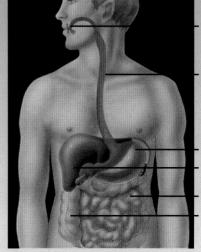

- mouth
- gullet
- stomach
- liver
- small intestine
- large intestine

📖 INSTANT FACTS

An average person eats about 500 kg **(half a tonne) of food each year.**

A joule is a measure of energy. Joules in foods are energy in chemical form. **A thousand joules are called kilojoules (kJ).**

The body uses this much energy, in kJ per minute, for:
Sitting quietly 6-7
Walking 15–20
Running 30-plus

Foods provide the following energy per gram: **Carbohydrate 16 kJ Protein 17 kJ Fat 35 kJ**

👁 HEALTHWATCH

Obesity is being overweight – a body which is too heavy for its height. It brings many health problems such as heart disease, clogged blood vessels, breathlessness, strained muscles and joint problems. Various fashionable diets come and go, but the main long-term aims are simple: eat less, exercise more.

For good health the body needs a range of different foods. It should not have too much of one food, and not too much of all foods either. Food substances fall into six main groups, and healthy amounts of all are called a balanced diet.

CARBOHYDRATES The body gets its energy from carbohydrates. They are broken down in the body into various sugars, especially glucose, a type of sugar, which is the body's main form of fast energy. Carbohydrates are found in bread, potatoes, parsnips and similar root crops, pastas, rice and other cereals, and various fruits and vegetables.

PROTEINS The body's main building materials are proteins. The protein we get from food is vital to maintain and repair body parts, and for growth in babies and children. Proteins occur in meat and fish, and also in milk, eggs, dairy products and some vegetables, especially peas and beans.

OILS & FATS Body parts like nerves get energy from oils and fats. Too much fat or oil from animal sources, especially fatty meats, can cause problems such as heart disease. Vegetables, fruits and seeds, like sunflower, corn and soya oils provide a much safer form of fats for the body.

VITAMINS & MINERALS Our bodies need vitamins and minerals in small but regular amounts to avoid illness. Iron, for example, is needed for making red blood cells which carry oxygen in the blood, while calcium helps keep teeth and bones strong, and nerves healthy. Vitamins and minerals are found in most foods, especially fresh fruit and vegetables.

FIBRE Many plant foods contain fibre. Although it is not absorbed by the body, fibre helps the intestines deal with food, and reduces the risk of digestive problems such as certain cancers. Fibre is found in wholegrain products like wholemeal bread, pasta and rice, fresh fruit, leafy vegetables and pulses like beans and lentils.

IN FOCUS
ENERGY VS NUTRIENTS

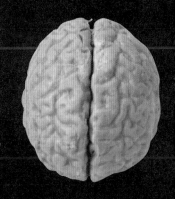

The brain uses far more energy for its size than any other body part. It consumes one-fifth of all energy in food, even though it makes up just one-fiftieth of the body's total weight.

MORE PEOPLE ARE BECOMING OVERWEIGHT in developed countries. Health experts describe this as an 'epidemic' since obesity raises the risks of many illnesses (see panel).

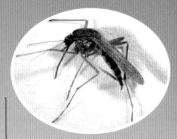

SOME ANIMALS HAVE A VERY SIMPLE DIET – BLOOD. Mosquitoes, vampire bats, leeches and fleas thrive on this all-round nutritious substance. Our own bodies are designed for a much wider range of foods.

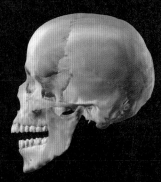

In contrast bones use just one-hundredth of the energy, weight for weight, compared to the brain. But they require from food a far greater proportion of minerals, especially calcium, phosphate and sulphate.

TRY IT YOURSELF

Look at a selection of foods with packaging and see how many joules they contain. Which foods do you think will be the healthiest for you?

FOOD GROUPS

Simple 'pie' charts colour-code food groups – high-protein meat and fish as yellow, sugar and starch as orange, fresh fruit and vegetables as red, bread and cereal as green and dairy products as blue. This helps to organise a balanced diet.

DIGESTION MOUTH & TEETH

The **first set of teeth** are called milk or deciduous teeth, and they number 20. Average ages for appearance, from front to back, are:

Front incisors 6–12 months.

Lateral (side) incisors 9–15 months.

Canines 15–24 months.

First premolars 15–20 months.

Second premolars 24–30 months.

After six or seven years, **the first teeth fall out** as the adult set of 32 teeth appear.

Look in a mirror, grin widely and poke out your tongue. You will see your digestive 'weapons'. Teeth cut and crush foods, while the tongue keeps food moving to make sure every piece is chewed thoroughly.*

TEETH AND SMILES The first set of teeth are the only parts of the body which fall out naturally, to be replaced by a second set. Each tooth has two parts, the crown showing above the gum and the root fixed firmly in the jawbone. Covering the crown is enamel, which is the body's hardest substance. Under this is dentine, which is slightly softer but still very tough. In the root the dentine is 'glued' into the jaw with a layer of cementum. Dentine absorbs knocks and shocks, otherwise chewing would be much more jarring and very noisy. In the centre of the tooth is the pulp of tiny blood vessels and nerves. The sensitive nerves are not just to detect toothache. They also warn of too much pressure when biting, since the whole tooth could crack or snap.

FOOD SCIENTISTS are always testing new flavours to 'tickle our palate', which really means to stimulate the tongue's taste buds.

HEALTHWATCH

Most people visit the dentist every 6–12 months. The dentist and hygienist advise on how to brush and use strands of floss to remove bits of food from between teeth. X-ray photographs reveal problems like cracks or cavities which cannot be seen on the outside.

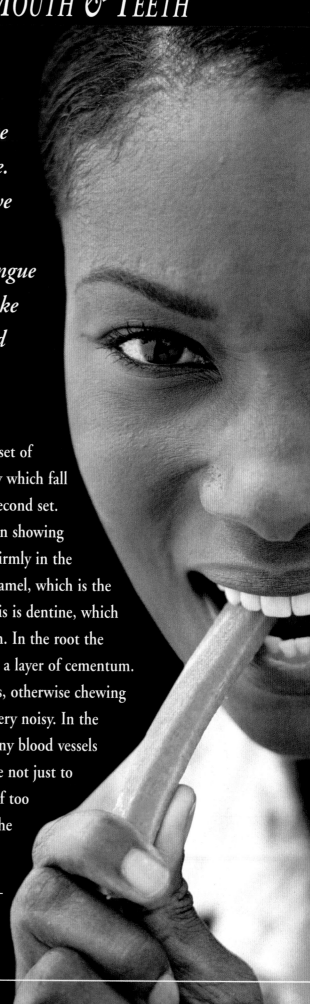

TEETH CAN GO THROUGH A LIFETIME OF WEAR AND TEAR, provided they are cleaned daily and checked regularly.

IN FOCUS
INSIDE A TOOTH

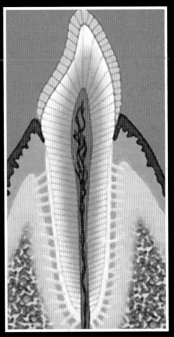

A cutaway canine tooth shows its tall pointed shape, outer enamel with dentine underneath, and delicate dental pulp. As we tear at food we put the canine under sideways stress so it has a root twice as long as its crown.

TASTY TONGUE If you try to eat very dry foods, your mouth soon feels rough and parched. This is because you run out of the watery liquid called saliva or spit. Three pairs of glands make around one and a half litres of saliva each day. On each side of the face the glands are below the ear, in the angle of the jaw and under the tongue. The tongue is almost all muscle – in fact, it's the most bendy muscle in the whole body. It pushes pieces of food between the teeth and holds them for crushing.

THE FRONT TEETH HAVE LONG THIN EDGES, designed to bite and cut mouth-sized chunks from larger food items.

TONSILS

The mouth is the way into the body not only for food and air, but also for germs. Two lumpy masses on either side of the lower tongue, the tonsils, are part of the body's immune defence system. They become swollen in tonsillitis.

tonsils

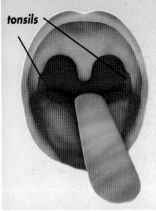

TRY IT YOURSELF

Open wide and look in a mirror to see the different shapes of your teeth. The front teeth, incisors, are sharp-edged for biting. Behind these are the taller, more pointed canines or 'eye teeth', for tearing. To the rear are the cheek teeth, premolars and molars, for squeezing and squashing. Some people have higher, more pointed canines than others.

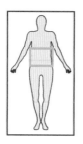

The stomach can enlarge to hold almost two litres of food.

The lining makes about **1.5 litres of gastric juices daily**.

This **lining also replaces itself compeletely** every three days.

There is an old saying: **'Your stomach shrinks if you eat smaller meals,** so you feel full with less food'. But unfortunately this is not true.

Eating too fast, especially when moving about or talking, can cause several problems. One is gulping down air with the food, which then has to come back – as a belch (burp). Another problem is heartburn. This is caused when too much stomach acid is sent up into the oesophagus, leading to a burning discomfort.

DIGESTION *Stomach*

The stomach is virtually in the centre of our bodies. It is very strong and muscular, and can stretch to hold a large meal. While food is in the stomach, it is mashed up and mixed with strong chemicals. By the time food leaves the stomach it is in the form of a thick liquid.

DOWN THE GULLET To swallow food, the back of the tongue pushes a lump of it into the top of the throat. Here the throat muscles 'grab' it and force it over a flap called the epiglottis. This folds down to prevent choking by stopping the food going into the windpipe. The muscles in the throat and then the gullet wall continue to push the food down through the neck and chest, by peristalsis. It takes just a few seconds for the food to reach the stomach.

THE STOMACH IS ON THE LEFT SIDE, with its centre about halfway between nipple and navel. As it expands with a meal its lower end can extend almost to the navel.

The stomach's hydrochloric acid is so strong that if it was made in a factory and put into bottles, it would need a warning label!

POISON

IN FOCUS
SWALLOWING

SQUEEZE AND SQUIRM The stomach is not just a stretchy bag that holds food before it passes to the next part of the digestive system. As it fills with a meal, the powerful layers of muscles in the stomach walls make it churn and squirm to squash the chewed food into a pulp. Also, the stomach's lining releases a watery liquid called gastric juice. This attacks the food with powerful chemicals called acids and enzymes. The 'acid bath' of hydrochloric acid in the stomach also helps to kill germs that came in with the food.

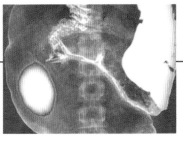

Barium is a substance that shows up as pale or white on X-rays. A barium meal fills the inside of the stomach and shows its shape and position, to reveal problems like tightness or constriction.

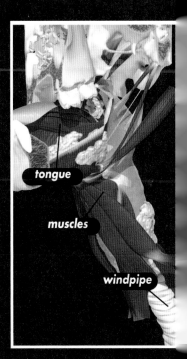

tongue

muscles

windpipe

The base of the tongue extends down into the neck and helps to push food into the gullet, which is behind the windpipe. The strap-like muscles around the upper windpipe and voicebox also help in swallowing.

TRY IT YOURSELF

Ask friends to point to where they think a stomach-ache would be. They may indicate around the navel (belly button). But you know better! The stomach is much higher, just behind the lower left ribs.

STOMACH WALL

The stomach lining has named regions and is wrinkled and folded (right). Around it are three layers of muscles, each with fibres arranged in different directions.

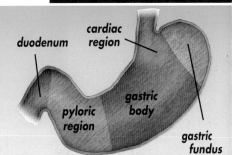

duodenum

cardiac region

pyloric region

gastric body

gastric fundus

The small intestine makes about **1.5 litres of digestive juices each day.**

Foods pass through the small intestine **for up to six hours.**

The lining has a total area which is **almost twice the skin area of the whole body.**

HEALTHWATCH

An easy way for harmful germs to spread is on foods. Some germs can withstand the acid attack in the stomach, and then multiply fast in the intestines, where they are surrounded by food. Washing hands before touching and preparing foods, and again before eating a meal, is an easy way to stop them.

DIGESTION *GUTS*

'Guts' can be any parts inside the body, especially digestive parts. But usually 'guts' mean the intestine and perhaps the stomach too. There is one small intestine and one large one.

NUTRIENTS INTO THE BODY On average, if a small intestine was straightened out, it would be seven times longer than the body it came from. The large intestine would be about the same length as the body's height. Mashed, pulped food from the stomach passes in small, regular 'squirts' through a muscular ring, the pyloric sphincter, into the small intestine. This has a lining which is covered with thousands of tiny finger-like parts, villi, each about one millimetre tall. The lining makes more enzymes and other chemicals to finish digesting the food. It also soaks up or absorbs the resulting nutrients, through the villi into the blood stream.

NEAR THE END The small intestine (small bowel) leads to the larger one, which is twice as wide.

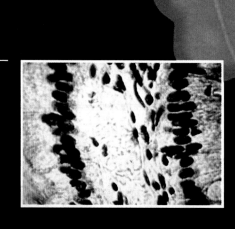

stomach

small intestine

large intestine

INSIDE A VILLUS ARE TINY TUBES OR VESSELS. *Some carry blood, which soaks up the nutrients from the digested food and carries them away around the body. The central tube is filled with lymph fluid, which also takes up nutrients.*

IN FOCUS
GUTS LARGE & SMALL

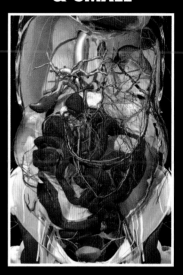

With the liver, stomach and large intestine out of the way, the small intestine is seen coiling its way around the lower half of the abdomen.

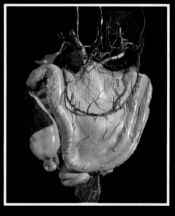

The guts are covered by a large sheet of fatty tissue, the omentum, which drapes like a curtain down the front of the abdomen.

OOOOOH, THE PAIN OF GUT-ACHE! This is sometimes due to eating too fast, when food is not chewed properly. Or it could be an infection from germs in food, or a blockage. An X-ray might show the intestines and whether they are swollen, or if food is piling up behind a blockage.

At the junction there is a finger-size part, the appendix. This is hollow inside but has a closed end and does not lead anywhere. Hard bits of food or germs sometimes get stuck in it and make it swell up, known as appendicitis. In the large intestine, water and minerals are taken from the leftover foods into the blood flowing through its lining. The leftovers become squishy, smelly, brown lumps or faeces. They are stored in the last part of the tract, the rectum, before removal through another ring of muscle, the anus, which also has several other names...

THE LARGE INTESTINE (LARGE BOWEL OR COLON) forms a 'picture frame' around the small one.

anus

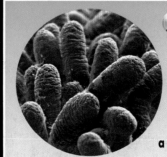

INTESTINAL VILLI

Like the stomach, the small intestine wall has several layers of muscle which make it squirm to push digested food along. The villi form a velvet-like surface inside, almost like a short-haired carpet.

15

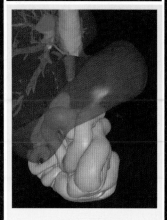
The liver is the body's **largest internal part, or organ**, with a weight of 1.5 kg.

The liver **makes almost one litre of bile daily**. It digests fat in a similar way to how detergents clean our washing up.

The liver contains **more blood, in proportion to its size**, than almost any other body part.

⊙ **HEALTHWATCH**

A yellow tinge to the skin and eyes is known as jaundice – and is often a sign of liver trouble. Usually the liver breaks down old red blood cells and gets rid of their colouring substance, or pigment, in bile fluid. If something goes wrong the colouring substance builds up in blood and skin and produces jaundice. Infection of the liver by various germs, in different types of hepatitis, can cause jaundice.

DIGESTION *Liver & Pancreas*

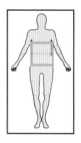

Some machines and people can 'multi-task' and do many jobs at once. Apart from the brain, the liver is the body's best multi-tasker. It has more than 500 jobs, mainly to do with body chemistry.

HUNDREDS OF JOBS The liver has two blood supplies. As well as the normal flow direct from the heart, there is another supply from the intestines, rich in nutrients. What the liver does with these nutrients depends on the body's needs. If blood-sugar levels are already high, the liver may change some of the glucose from digestion into starch. It then stores this starch, known as glycogen, for later times when energy supplies are low. The same storage-or-release happens with many other substances, including vitamins.

The toxins (poisons) which the liver makes harmless include drugs such as alcohol. But too much alcohol overloads the liver and causes the very serious disease known as cirrhosis.

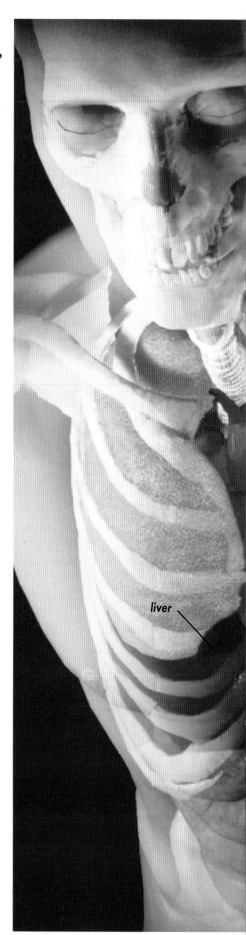

liver

stomach

One of the liver's most important tasks is 'detox'. This is detoxification, breaking apart toxins or poisonous substances. The liver also makes a liquid, bile, which is stored in a small bag beneath it, the gall bladder. After a meal, bile flows along the bile duct into the small intestine, where it helps to digest fatty foods.

TWO JOBS In contrast to the liver, the pancreas has only two main tasks. One is to make strong digestive juices containing enzymes. After a meal, these ooze along the pancreatic ducts into the small intestine, where they aid digestion. The pancreas's other main task is to produce hormones.

The wedge-shaped liver extends at its right side from the level of the nipple almost down to the waist. In this position it is partly protected by the lower right ribs. The pancreas lies just below the stomach, hidden away.

👋 TRY IT YOURSELF

If you know any babies or toddlers, take a look at their bulging tummies. It is not the stomach which causes this natural bulge – it is the liver. Compared to an adult, a baby's liver is much larger in proportion to the rest of the body. It takes up almost half the entire abdomen, but only one-quarter in a grown-up.

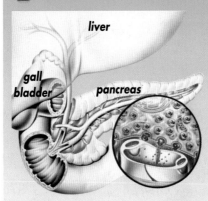

🔧 INSIDE THE PANCREAS AND LIVER

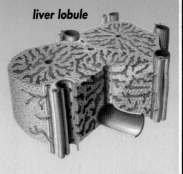

liver lobule

liver

gall bladder

pancreas

Within the pancreas (left) are tiny bunches of cells that make digestive juices. There are also cells which make hormones. The liver (right) has thousands of six-sided, blob-like units called lobules, each about one millimetre across.
A lobule has its own blood vessels and also tubes for bile (shown in green) which goes to the gall bladder.

IN FOCUS
UPPER ABDOMEN

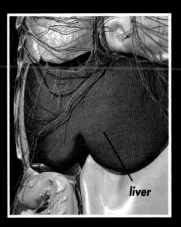

liver

The liver is pressed up against the base of the chest, with most of its bulk on the body's right side. It is dark red in colour due to its massive blood content.

pancreas

With the liver and stomach out of the way, the pancreas is seen lying across the abdomen, over the two kidneys. It is soft and grey-pink, with ducts leading from its blunt right end or 'head' into the small intestine.

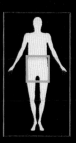

On a hot day when rushing about, you may not need the toilet for hours. On a cold day with little action, you may need it ten times. This difference is due to the way the body balances its inputs of foods and drinks, and its outputs of various wastes - especially the liquid waste we call urine.

FILTERING THE BLOOD The body gets rid of wastes in gas, solid and liquid forms. A waste gas called carbon dioxide leaves from the lungs every time we breathe out. Waste solids leave once or twice daily, as faeces, while the waste liquid urine leaves a number of times. Urine is made by the the kidneys, which are two organs in the back of the upper abdomen. For its size, each kidney has a massive blood flow. Inside the kidney are about one million micro-filters known as nephrons. They remove unwanted substances from blood along with water which the body does not need, as urine.

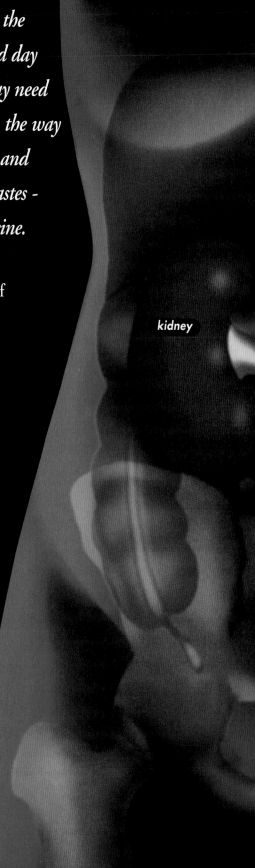

kidney

SOME ANIMALS USE THEIR WASTES TO MARK THEIR TERRITORIES, *leaving piles of dung and spraying urine.*

IN FOCUS
KIDNEYS AND BLADDER

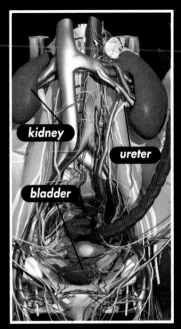

kidney

ureter

bladder

The kidneys' huge blood supply is shown by the size of the renal arteries (red) and veins (blue). The pale ureter tubes lead down to the bladder.

THE KIDNEYS ARE QUITE HIGH IN THE ABDOMEN, against its back wall, shielded by the lower ribs. The left one is usually slightly higher than the right. The bladder is in the front base of the abdomen. In this picture the kidneys have been brought to the front of the body so you can see clearly where they are.

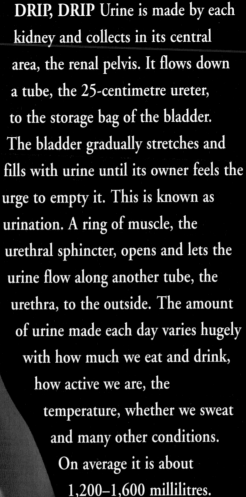

ureter

kidney

bladder

urethra

DRIP, DRIP Urine is made by each kidney and collects in its central area, the renal pelvis. It flows down a tube, the 25-centimetre ureter, to the storage bag of the bladder. The bladder gradually stretches and fills with urine until its owner feels the urge to empty it. This is known as urination. A ring of muscle, the urethral sphincter, opens and lets the urine flow along another tube, the urethra, to the outside. The amount of urine made each day varies hugely with how much we eat and drink, how active we are, the temperature, whether we sweat and many other conditions. On average it is about 1,200–1,600 millilitres.

TRY IT YOURSELF

Next time you are active on a hot day, add up how much fluid you drink. Is it more than the usual two or so litres? Most of this extra water is lost as sweat. Drinking lots on a cooler day means more water leaves the body in urine, making its colour paler than normal.

KIDNEY MICRO-FILTERS

Each tiny nephron has a ball-shaped knot of capillary blood vessels, the glomerulus. This is surrounded by a cup-shaped capsule which extends into a long, looped tube. Wastes, minerals and water pass from the blood into the tube. Here useful minerals and some water are taken back into the blood, leaving urine.

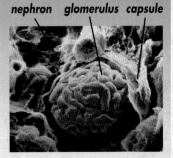

nephron   glomerulus   capsule

There are many examples of hormones:

Insulin is made by the pancreas, which lies beneath the stomach. It controls the **way our bodies use the sugar, glucose.**

Adrenaline is the hormone which is **released when we become frightened or stressed.** It is named after the adrenal gland, from which it comes.

Thyroxine is an important hormone which **affects just about every part of the body.** It tells the tissues how fast to work.

👁 HEALTHWATCH

Several hormones need regular supplies of certain minerals in food. One is iodine, for the thyroid to make thyroxine. In many regions tiny amounts of iodine are added to table salt and cooking salt, and a healthy diet contains enough in any case. But if iodine is severely lacking in food, the thyroid become larger as it tries to make enough thyroxine. The result is a swelling in the neck called a goitre.

DIGESTION *In Control*

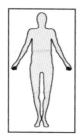

As well as being controlled by the brain through the nervous system, the tissues of your body get instructions from special chemicals in the blood called hormones. These hormones, and the glands which produce them, make up the endocrine system.

TWO SYSTEMS The body has two control systems. The brain and nerves send nerve signals around the body to control its muscles, heartbeat, breathing and many other rapid-action processes. The other control system takes longer to react but also lasts longer. This is the endocrine or hormonal system, using natural chemicals called hormones, made in parts known as endocrine glands. Hormones are released into the blood and travel around the body to affect certain parts, known as targets, usually making them work faster or slower.

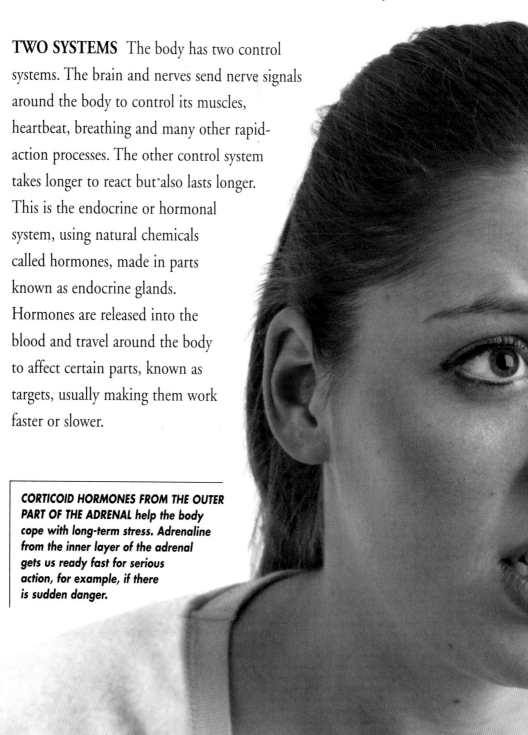

CORTICOID HORMONES FROM THE OUTER PART OF THE ADRENAL help the body cope with long-term stress. Adrenaline from the inner layer of the adrenal gets us ready fast for serious action, for example, if there is sudden danger.

IN FOCUS
HORMONAL GLANDS

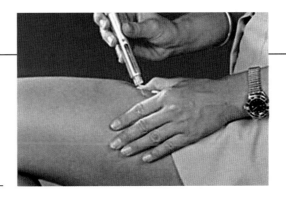

IN THE CONDITION KNOWN AS 'DIABETES' THERE IS A PROBLEM MAKING THE HORMONE INSULIN. People with diabetes may have to inject insulin into their bodies every day of their lives.

SMALL BUT IMPORTANT There are more than 100 hormones. About ten come from the pea-sized pituitary, just under the front of the brain. These include the growth hormone, which regulates the body's long-term development, and several hormones that control other hormone-making glands like the thyroid and adrenals. Thyroxine hormone from the thyroid controls the body's rate of energy use and general 'speed' of inner processes.

The adrenal glands are shown here as lumpy, pale, curved triangles, seen from the body's rear. They are also called the supra-renal glands, because there is one on top of each kidney.

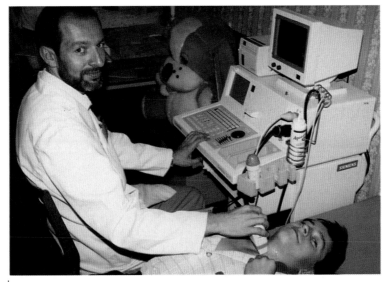

The thyroid is in the front of the neck. Its main hormone, thyroxine, contains the mineral iodine (see Healthwatch). This patient is having his thyroid examined by a doctor.

The thyroid gland wraps around the front of the upper windpipe, just below the voicebox. It is pale and almost X-shaped, its wide left and right lobes joined by a narrower middle section.

TRY IT YOURSELF

Next time you are suddenly startled or surprised, check your pulse. The hormone adrenaline will be at work, making your heart beat faster as more blood flows to your muscles, ready for action. Less blood goes to your stomach and intestines, causing 'butterflies in the tummy'.

SEX HORMONES

Males and females produce different hormones which make their bodies change during puberty. Testosterone is the male hormone and is made by the testes. In females oestrogen and progesterone are produced by the ovaries. These hormones are all necessary for reproduction.

INSTANT FACTS

In females, **each ovary is 3 cm long** and 1.5 cm wide— hardly the size of a thumb.

In an woman's **average lifetime about 400–500 egg cells are released** in total, from a store of 200,000 in each ovary.

In a male, each testis is about 5 cm long and 2.5 cm wide, and **makes many thousands of sperm cells every second.**

👁 HEALTHWATCH

The production of eggs or sperm can be affected in many ways, including unhealthy diet, lack of sleep, worry and stress, and drugs such as alcohol. If eggs do not ripen in a woman, or sperm numbers are low in a man, then a couple who wish to have a baby may have problems. This is known as low fertility. Often, advice from the doctor, and perhaps some simple treatment, can solve the problem.

Waaaaaah! Babies can be very noisy and tiring to look after. But we need them to carry on humankind. Reproduction is making more of your kind. A body is either female or male depending on which reproductive parts it has.

FEMALE & EGGS The ovaries are in either side of the lower abdomen. Each month or so, one of them produces a tiny, ripe egg cell. Over several days this egg makes its way along a tube, the oviduct (Fallopian tube), towards the womb. If nothing happens to it then it passes out of the body, along with the blood-rich lining of the womb, through the vagina (birth canal), as the menstrual flow or period. The whole process, the menstrual cycle, then begins again, under the control of several hormones. But if the egg cell meets a sperm cell, the two get together to begin the reproductive process.

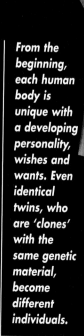

From the beginning, each human body is unique with a developing personality, wishes and wants. Even identical twins, who are 'clones' with the same genetic material, become different individuals.

IN FOCUS
OVARIES & SPERM

REPRODUCTION IS A BASIC PROCESS that occurs in all living things, plants and animals. In humans it also involves feelings of affection, friendship, love and desire–which can become very complicated!

MALE & SPERM Tadpole-shaped sperm are produced all the time in long tubes known as seminiferous tubules. These are coiled in the two testes, which hang below the front abdomen in a skin bag, the scrotum. The sperm are stored in another long tube, the epididymis, next to each testis. During sex they leave the body in a fluid which passes along another tube, the vas deferens, and then through a gland, the prostate, and along yet another tube, the urethra, which runs through the penis to the outside.

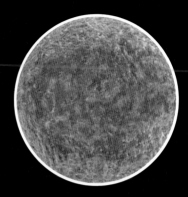

In the ovary, an egg grows and becomes ripe inside a small fluid bag, the follicle. About halfway through the cycle the follicle breaks open and the egg is released, or ovulated, into the oviduct.

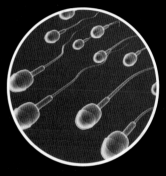

In the testes, sperm begin as blob-shaped spermatocytes, around the inner edge of each seminiferous tubule. Over ten weeks they grow tails and become ripe or mature sperm, in the middle of the tubule.

REPRODUCTIVE SYSTEMS

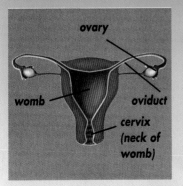

ovary
womb
oviduct
cervix (neck of womb)

THE OVARIES are slightly above and behind the womb. They are held in position in the lower abdomen by strap-like ligaments. The oviducts curl around and down, and lead to the womb, or uterus. This is shaped like a forward-tilted pear.

THE TESTES are below the abdomen, and so slightly cooler than the main body. Sperm production is affected by temperature – too warm and fewer sperm are formed. This would happen if the testes were like the ovaries, within the abdomen.

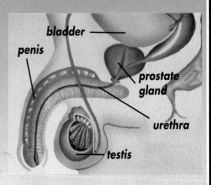

bladder
penis
prostate gland
urethra
testis

Three weeks after fertilisation the tiny heart is pulsing. Length is 2.5 mm.

After four weeks the eyes, arms and legs start to grow. Length is 5 mm.

After five weeks the brain enlarges greatly and the nose, mouth and intestines are growing. Length is 8 mm.

After six weeks the ears and eyes begin to take shape, the arms lengthen and there is still a tail. Length is 12 mm.

👁 HEALTHWATCH

The mother's health is very important to the growing embryo. It can be harmed if she smokes tobacco, drinks too much alcohol, or takes certain drugs, or lacks nutrients in her food. Even some medical drugs should not be taken during pregnancy. Certain diseases in the mother also affect the embryo's development, such as rubella (german measles).

REPRODUCTION *THE BODY BEGINS*

There are more than 6,000 million bodies in the world, and they all began in the same way. A tiny egg cell and an even tinier sperm cell came together and joined. The same process is happening now, more than three times each second, to make babies that will be born in nine months' time.

IN THE TUBE As a just-released egg cell drifts slowly along the oviduct of the female system, it may suddenly meet thousands of sperm cells coming the other way. They have completed a very long journey out of the man's body, into the woman's and through the womb. Only one of the sperm joins, or fertilises, the egg. This brings together the genetic material from mother and father, which contains all the instructions needed for a new human body to grow and develop. The fertilised egg cell continues to drift along but within a day it splits or divides into two cells, then four, eight and so on. This is the early embryo stage.

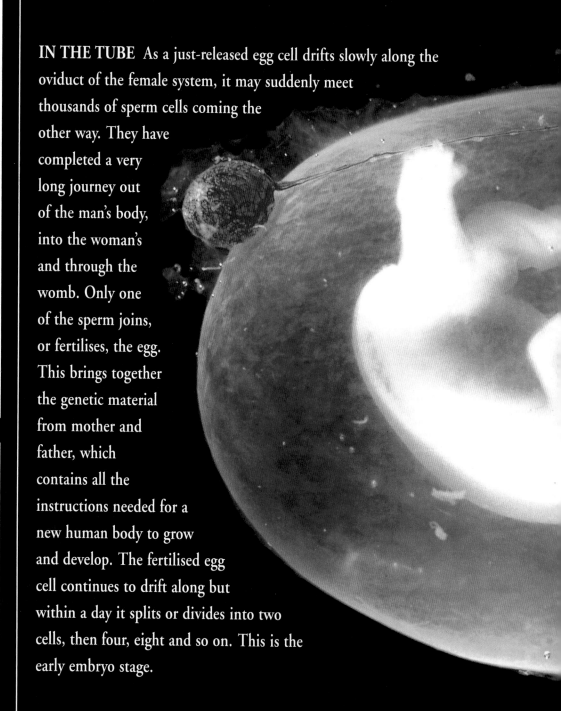

IN THE WOMB About a week after fertilisation the tiny early embryo, as small as the dot on this i, settles into the lining of the womb. The lining has become rich in blood and nutrients as part of the menstrual cycle. The cells of the embryo continue to divide, move about and change shape as they evolve into the cells of body parts like nerves, brain, muscles, and blood. Eight weeks after fertilisation the embryo has become a miniature human body, hardly bigger than a grape, with all its main body parts formed.

Immediately after fertilisation a human egg shows no signs of developing into an embryo.

After 2-3 days the embryo's cells start to divide.

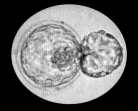

After around six days, the embryo 'hatches' out just before implanting in the wall of the uterus.

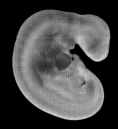

After it has attached to the uterus, the embryo continues to grow, taking on a more recognisable form. This embryo is about four weeks old.

About seven weeks after fertilisation the embryo floats in its amniotic bag of fluid. The yolk sac which provided nourishment during earlier stages has shrunk to a tiny 'balloon'.

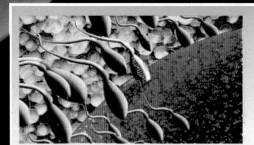

SPERM MEETS EGG

The sperm is tiny compared to the egg. Its genetic material is in the rounded head end which burrows through the outer layer of the egg, so the male and female genetic material can come together.

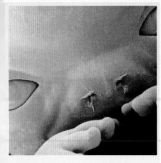
After **four months the baby's bones begin to harden** and the teeth start to grow as tiny 'buds' under the gums. Girls can be told apart from boys.

After **six months the stomach and intestines are fully formed**, the nostrils open and the baby may suck its thumb.

After **eight months fat collects under the skin** but overall growth starts to slow down. The baby has a good chance of survival if born.

Antenatal check-ups are very important for the expectant mother. She receives an examination and also tests such as heart rate and blood pressure. Sometimes problems of pregnancy do not cause obvious symptoms until well advanced. The medical check helps to detect them early, so treatment can be started straight away.

REPRODUCTION *Towards Birth*

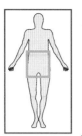

From eight weeks after it began, until the time of birth, the developing baby is known as a fetus. Most of this time is spent growing larger and adding finishing details to the body, like hair and nails.

GROWTH IN THE WOMB In the womb, the baby grows in length by more than 10 times in seven months. It floats in liquid called amniotic fluid inside the womb. At first it can wave its arms and kick its legs, and even turn somersaults. But later the fetus becomes cramped and can move less. In the middle of pregnancy the baby is slim and wrinkled. Towards the end it puts on fat under the skin so it looks more chubby.

THE GREAT DAY After nine months the baby is ready to be born. The muscles in the wall of the womb tighten during contractions and gradually push the baby out, through the cervix (opening or neck of the womb). The baby then passes along the vagina or birth canal, to the outside. Birth can take many hours and is hugely tiring for both mother and baby.

THE MOTHER'S ABDOMEN BEGINS TO BULGE after about four months of the nine-month pregnancy. She usually attends antenatal ('before birth') checks, to make sure she and the developing baby are well.

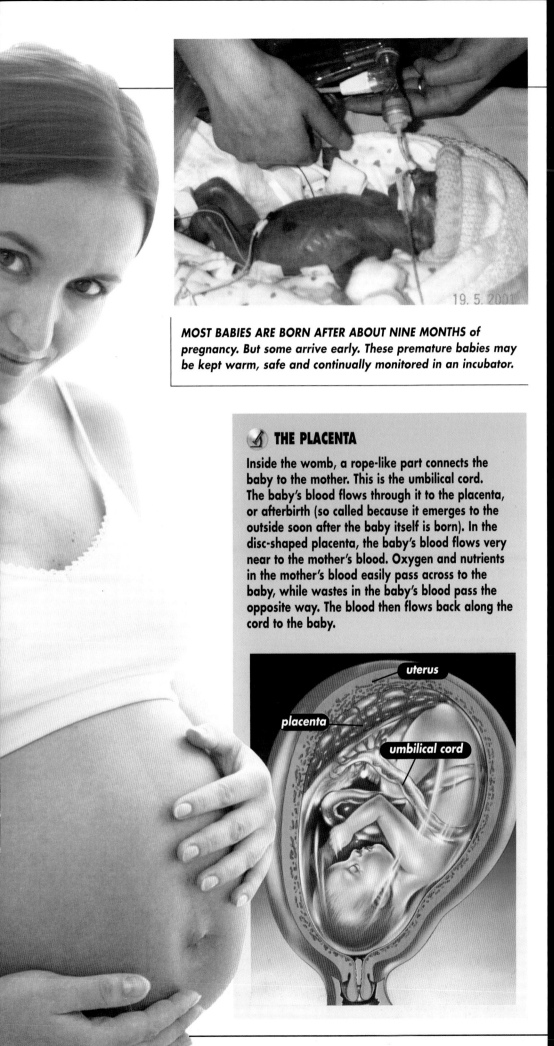

MOST BABIES ARE BORN AFTER ABOUT NINE MONTHS of pregnancy. But some arrive early. These premature babies may be kept warm, safe and continually monitored in an incubator.

THE PLACENTA

Inside the womb, a rope-like part connects the baby to the mother. This is the umbilical cord. The baby's blood flows through it to the placenta, or afterbirth (so called because it emerges to the outside soon after the baby itself is born). In the disc-shaped placenta, the baby's blood flows very near to the mother's blood. Oxygen and nutrients in the mother's blood easily pass across to the baby, while wastes in the baby's blood pass the opposite way. The blood then flows back along the cord to the baby.

uterus

placenta

umbilical cord

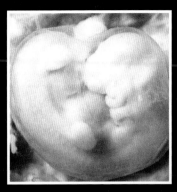

After just a few weeks, the fetus starts to take on a human appearance, with hands, feet and head recognisable.

After several months, the fetus's body becomes tubbier and covered in a creamy substance, vernix, which stops the skin from becoming waterlogged.

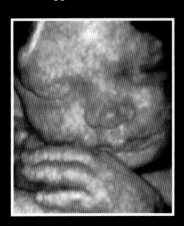

By 8–9 months the fetus is ready to be born. The average weight of a baby at birth is 3–3.5 kg.

Our knowledge of the body's health, diet, illness and treatment has meant huge advances in the length and quality of our lives.

Children of today are about 2 cm taller, for the same age, than children of 100 years ago.

In most developed countries, the average lifespan for people born 200 years ago was about 30–35 years.

During the teenage years, smallish problems can be hugely worrying – even when almost everyone has them. One common condition is the spots of acne, especially on the face and neck. These can be treated by extra-careful washing and hygiene, and various creams and lotions. Picking spots may infect them with germs so they become worse than ever.

REPRODUCTION *BABY TO ADULT*

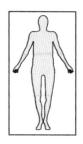

Most people do not reach their full body height until about 20 years. Greatest muscle power may occur a few years later. But growing up is not only physical. Also important is how we behave, learn new information, take decisions, make friends and get on with other people.

INFANCY & CHILDHOOD From the moment of birth the new baby learns at an amazing rate. It learns the sounds, sights and smells of its mother and family. From about six weeks it learns that if it smiles, other people smile back and play with it, which is less boring than lying alone. From about five months a typical baby can sit up, then at eight months crawl, and 11–12 months walk. These actions and movements are called motor skills. Most babies develop them in the same order but the ages differ widely.

THE NEWBORN BABY IS NOT ENTIRELY 'HELPLESS'. It has built-in reactions or instincts to cry when hungry, hot, cold, damp or uncomfortable – such as when its nappy needs changing.

FROM THE AGE OF ABOUT TWO, young children want to find out and explore. But they do not understand about danger. This can often lead to a battle of wills which ends in the temper tantrums of the 'terrible twos'.

CHILD TO ADULT At the age of two years, most toddlers are about half as tall as they will be when they are adults. But their weight is only one-fifth of their expected adult weight. During childhood, growth gradually slows down. Then from about 9–12 years in girls, and a couple of years later in boys, growth speeds up again and the body changes in shape and features. The reproductive parts enlarge and begin to work, during the time known as puberty. In boys this takes up to four years, in girls about two or three years.

During the teenage years, many people spend less time with their close family and more with others of their own age. Friendships can become very intense, very fast – then fade just as quickly.

GROWING UP FAST

Until puberty, girls and boys have similar body sizes and outlines. During puberty the average male body grows taller and more angular, with broader shoulders, increased muscle, facial hair (see left) and a much deeper or 'broken' voice. The average female body grows not quite so tall, and becomes more rounded with wider hips, developed breasts, and a slightly deeper voice.

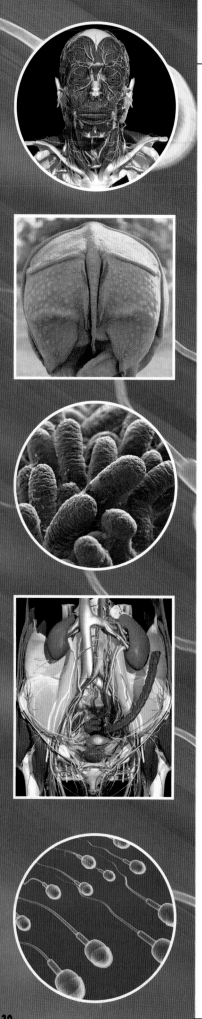

ABDOMEN The lower main body, from the base of the chest down to the hips, which contains the main parts for digestion, waste disposal and reproduction.

APPENDIX A small, finger-like, dead-end branch from the start of the large intestine, in the lower right of the abdomen.

ARTERY Strong, thick-walled main blood vessel that carries blood away from the heart. Note: Not all arteries carry bright red, high-oxygen blood. The two umbilical arteries from the unborn baby to the placenta convey dark, low-oxygen 'blue' blood.

BALANCED DIET A suitable selection of varied foods that keeps the body healthy and minimises the risks of various diseases.

BLADDER A bag- or sac-like body part, usually meaning the urinary bladder which stores urine made by the kidneys.

CAPILLARY The thinnest, shortest type of blood vessel, far too narrow to see with the naked eye.

CARTILAGE A strong, smooth, shiny, slightly bendy substance, sometimes called 'gristle', that forms body parts like the nose, ears and voicebox, and covers the ends of bones in a joint.

CARBON DIOXIDE A waste product made inside the body by releasing the energy from food substances, which is carried in the blood and passes into the air in the lungs, to be breathed out.

CELLS Tiny parts or building-blocks of the body, which in their billions make up larger parts like bones, muscles and skin.

COLON Another name for most of the large intestine.

DEHYDRATION Lack of water, which in the body can cause serious problems in just a few hours.

DENTINE A tough substance under the enamel coating of a tooth, resembling the 'ivory' of an elephant tusk.

ENAMEL The whitish or pale yellow covering of a tooth – enamel is the hardest substance in the body.

ENDOCRINE GLAND A hormone-making gland. It does not have a tube or duct to carry away its product, but releases the hormone directly into the blood flowing through the gland.

ENZYMES Substances which speed up or slow down the rate of chemical processes and changes. Digestive enzymes speed the breakdown of food in the stomach and intestines.

EXCRETION The removal of unwanted substances and wastes from the body.

GALL BLADDER A small bag behind the liver on the lower right, which stores the fluid bile made by the liver and passes it into the small intestine.

GASTRIC To do with the stomach.

HEPATIC To do with the liver.

HORMONE A natural substance made in the body by an endocrine gland, which circulates in the blood and controls a certain process or change.

LIGAMENT A strong, slightly stretchy part shaped like a strap or cord, which holds together bones at a joint, allowing them to move to a certain extent but not too much.

MINERALS Simple substances, many of which are metals in pure form, needed by the body to work well and stay healthy. They include iron, calcium, iodine, sodium and potassium.

MUSCLE A body part that contracts to help the body move.

NEPHRONS Tiny filtering units in the kidney which remove unwanted substances and excess water from blood to form urine.

PERISTALSIS Moving waves or constrictions of muscles along a tube-like body part, squeezing along its contents, such as food in the gut or urine in the ureter.

RENAL To do with the kidneys.

UMBILICAL CORD The rope-like part linking the unborn baby to the placenta or afterbirth in the wall of the womb.

URETER Tube conveying urine from the kidney to the bladder.

URETHRA Tube conveying urine from the bladder to the outside.

UTERUS The womb, the female reproductive part where a baby grows and develops before birth.

VEIN Wide but thin-walled main blood vessel that carries blood back to the heart. Note: Not all veins carry dark, low-oxygen 'blue' blood. The umbilical vein from the placenta to the unborn baby conveys bright red, high-oxygen blood.

VITAMINS Substances needed in small amounts for the body to stay healthy and work well. Many are found in fresh fruits and vegetables, and some, such as vitamin D, can be made by the body.

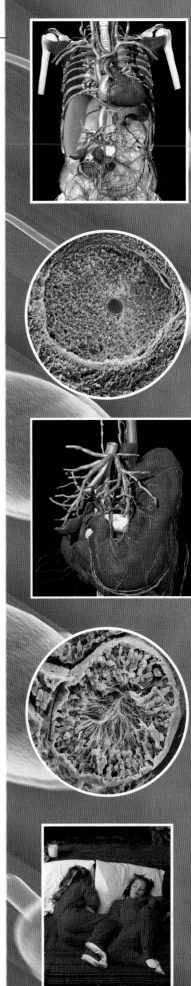

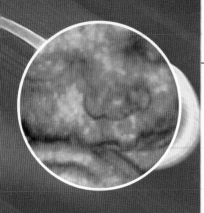

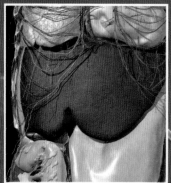

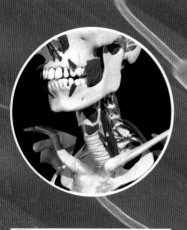

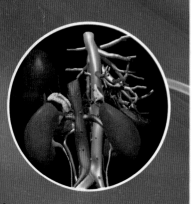

Copyright © ticktock Entertainment Ltd 2004
First published in Great Britain in 2004 by ticktock Media Ltd.,
Unit 2, Orchard Business Centre, North Farm Road, Tunbridge Wells, Kent, TN2 3XF
We would like to thank: Elizabeth Wiggans and Jenni Rainford for their help with this book.
ISBN 1 86007 563 0 HB   ISBN 1 86007 559 2 PB
Printed in China
A CIP catalogue record for this book is available from the British Library.

Picture Credits
Alamy: OFCl, 8-9c, 10tl, 10-11c, 11t, 11b, 29c, 29bc. Creatas: 12-13c. Primal Pictures: 7tr, 13tr, 15tr, 15br, 16tl, 17tr, 17cr, 19tr, 21tr, 21cr. Science Photo Library: 4-5c, 7br, 13t, 14-15c, 16-17c, 17bc, 17br, 18-19c, 19br, 21br, 23tr, 23br, 26tl, 27b. Wellcome Photo Library: 25r all.